IMPROVE YOUR BUSINESS RELATIONSHIPS

...How to Ensure Your Business Relationships Are Good for Your Business

By

Mark Sanchez

LEGAL DISCLAIMER

This document is geared towards providing exact and reliable information in regards to the topic and issue covered. The publication is sold with the idea that the publisher is not required to render accounting, officially permitted, or otherwise, qualified services. If advice is necessary, legal or professional, a practiced individual in the profession should be ordered.

In no way is it legal to reproduce, duplicate, or transmit any part of this document in either electronic means or in printed format. Recording of this publication is strictly prohibited and any storage of this document is not allowed unless with written permission from the publisher. All rights reserved.

The information provided herein is stated to be truthful and consistent, in that any liability, in terms of inattention or otherwise, by any usage or abuse of any policies, processes, or directions contained within is the solitary and utter responsibility of the recipient reader.

Under no circumstances will any legal responsibility or blame be held against the publisher for any reparation, damages, or monetary loss due to the information herein, either directly or indirectly.

Respective authors own all copyrights not held by the publisher.

The information herein is offered for informational purposes solely, and is universal as so. The presentation of the information is without contract or any type of guarantee assurance.

The trademarks that are used are without any consent, and the publication of the trademark is without permission or backing by the trademark owner. All trademarks and brands within this book are for clarifying purposes only and are the owned by the owners themselves, not affiliated with this document.

TABLE OF CONTENTS

INTRODUCTION

Hello,

Thank you for downloading this amazing guide—**"IMPROVE YOUR BUSINESS RELATIONSHIPS: How to Ensure Your Business Relationships Are Good for Your Business."**

People who market their business successfully on the Internet will tell you that good relationship do end up as good outcomes. If you are asking yourself how you can improve your business during these tough economic times, think about spending more time developing relationships.

An excellent place to start is to figure out what was the one area that you gained the best return on your investment in time. Then explore what the target market would be just for that one area. Your next step will then be to make a list of ways in which you can be introduced or referred to that target market.

Some possible ways to increase your exposure to your target market may include joining civic or business groups such as your local chambers or rotary club. It may be by joining your local BNI (Business Network International) or some other business networking group. And it may be by becoming more active in your local professional group.

When you do join these groups keep in mind that it is the little things that count. For instance, don't be on time for the meeting, arrive a little early and network. When you show up barely on time or late you are sending a message that you are not organised and that this group is not as talented as the reason you're late.

Sometimes we get so busy we forget about doing this, but it works. If you give someone in the group a referral, call them up and see how it is going. Maybe it didn't work out, and you have another source that will. If someone gives you a referral provide that member with an update about how it's going.

When you follow up on referrals, you give and get it sends an important message to your colleagues. You are telling them that you value them, their time and effort. The chances are excellent that you will receive more referrals.

Another strategy that brings success is giving testimonials to your business colleagues. It is incredible that just saying a few words, particularly at a meeting, can generate the possibility of so much additional business.

The reason is that when you give testimonials about others, it makes them feel good because it provides that person with more credibility. The credibility and trust that you've given that person are far better than anything he could say about himself. One good testimonial in the right place and time can be more valuable than a new client.

You can give a testimonial to someone after you've done business with that person, met with that person and spoke to his customers or clients, helped someone you know, observed how well he worked for another organisation.

The key is to keep testimonials brief.

Relationships are based on trust and take time. Support other people and they will support you.

Let's Get Started!

IMPROVE YOUR BUSINESS RELATIONSHIPS

AR YOU SPENDING TIM WITH TH 'RIGHT' PEOPLE?

You are the average of the 5 people you spend the most time with.

You may have heard this quote before but do you pay heed? Stop for a moment to think about this: it can be argued that all the most important aspects of your life - your dreams, aspirations, energy, contribution, relationships, feelings of success, health, financial situation etc. are likely to be a reflection of the average of the 5 people you spend most of your time with!

Concerning your business performance, it could well be worth spending ten minutes (or an hour!) examining who your influences are and the potential impact of these relationships on your business performance.

Follow this 4 step process to make sure that the top 5 people you currently spend most of your time with are positive for your performance in business (and of course, in life!).

1. Identify WHO your top 5 business relationships are.

In your business life, who are the top 5 people and organisations you spend time with? Brainstorm all the people and organisations you spend time with - and get creative. It includes people you see face to face, those you think about, people you email, individuals who make you feel stressed! These could be your business partner, employees, people you share office space with, clients, suppliers, mentors, competitors, even websites you spend a LOT of time on.

Once you have them all there, circle the top 5 - the key individuals you spend most of your time 'with'.

2. What is the IMPACT of these particular relationships?

Think about the following for each of your top 5:

For what reason does this relationship exist? Why do you spend so much time with or thinking about this person?

What sorts of emotions and experiences do these people generate for you? What energy do they have? How do you feel following interactions with this person?

Are they inspiring and motivating? Do they generate passion and creativity?

Are their values aligned with yours? Or are they focused on areas that conflict with your priorities?

What types of conversations are you having with these people?

Does your work and time spent with these people help to fuel the passion you have for your work?

Do these individuals and businesses have attributes that you want to possess yourself? Or are they in the same place as you, reinforcing where you are currently at, rather than where you would like to be?

3. Take stock of the impact of these working relationships on your business performance.

Bearing in mind what you have come up with in step 2, and your goals and aspirations for your business and your working life, take the time now to determine whether these relationships are right for you and your business or not.

How does your current business performance reflect your top 5?

Can you see any link between the current performance of your business and those top 5 relationships?

Maybe you are achieving huge success and surround yourself with like-minded people who support you to push yourself. Perhaps you can recognise that you have some fundamental relationships that sap a lot of your energy, leaving you drained and unable to hold yourself to the high standards you aspire to.

Do you have clients who you work with out of obligation rather than exact alignment?

Is each relationship taking you and your business to where you want to be, or merely affirming your current position? Can you recognise that you are holding yourself and your business back by continually associating with individuals and organisations who are at the same place as you are, rather than with people who have already achieved the success you aspire to? Or maybe these individuals and businesses have attributes that you want to possess yourself, and by being in a relationship with them, you are setting yourself up for success.

Use this step to identify those relationships that are positively impacting on your business performance, but also to determine which relationships are holding you back, inhibiting your progress, or negatively affecting on your return.

And let's be clear - not every relationship should be examined with a mindset of 'what can I get out of this' or 'how could this person benefit my business', but it is important to surround yourself with positive influences whether that's people who challenge you to learn and grow, mentors who inspire you to be your best or just people who allow you to express your creativity and passion for your work.

4. Use this knowledge to IMPROVE your business performance.

Now that you have identified where your relationships are supporting you and which ones are holding you back take action! What can you do to enhance those relationships that are positive for you and your business? How can you ensure you nurture those relationships and that you continue to soak up the positives?

Where there is room to step it up, get clear on what kind of people you do what to be surrounding yourself with and to seek them out. If you have specific aims or goals, which groups or individuals could you align yourself with so you can be with people who share your values and vision.

If you need development in a particular area, there are others in this zone congregating? Perhaps it's a matter of joining a business forum, development or networking group so you can meet these like-minded people.

AND - who do you need to distance yourself from? Perhaps you have clients who are draining your energy and sapping your passion for your work. Is it in your interests to create closure on that relationship so you can create space for clients who you feel a passion for working with?

Similarly, if you are experiencing painful or harmful relationships with suppliers or even employees - what course of action could you take to get these relationships to a point where they are positive for you and your business?

If you have a strong desire to improve your business performance work through these four steps to ensure your interactions and relationships in business are not only inspirational and fulfilling but take your business to the next level.

DVLING AND MINTINING BUSINSS

You may be one of the fortunate few who builds relationships - whether business or personal quickly and naturally. If so, more power to you. If not, take heart. You're in very good company. Developing and maintaining strong business relationships takes planning, reflection and practice. Here are a few guidelines to help you stay on track:

- **Be honest**. Be truthful and straightforward at every turn. Of course, this means you will sometimes have to offer negative feedback. It won't always be easy. Nevertheless, openness in your business dealings merely is non-negotiable.

- **Be flexible**. Whether you're dealing with a direct report, a colleague or a client, find ways to honour reasonable requests for latitude and accommodation.

- **Be gracious**. Use kindness and compassion in your business dealings even when the stakes are high. It's not only the right thing to do, but it's also smart business.

- **Be interested**. Ask your business associates how things are going. Without prying, convey your interest in their lives. Your genuine interest in others will help promote trust, communication and collaboration - all of which are vital for effective working relationships.

- Be generous. Freely offer your time, attention and expertise. Don't worry that others will take advantage of your generosity. More often than not, you will reap great rewards for your ungrudging generosity.

SIMPLE TACTICS TO IMPROVE YOUR BUSINESS

Whether you have a business of your own or are in employment, business relationships are just as meaningful as your relationships. You spend most of your waking hours at work, so you need to make sure that you put some effort into your business relationships or your working life will become not just miserable, but very unproductive.

RELATIONSHIP ROI

Have you ever heard of "Relationship ROI"? If you're not aware of ROI, it's an acronym for "Return On Investment".

Relationship ROI is all about the emphasis on the investment you are making in your business relationships and how much of an impact they can have on the success of your business dealings.

If you create and develop good business relationships then the return on that investment will be vast and far-reaching, so here are 10 tips that will help you with developing those relationships:

1. First impressions

First impressions count, so you need to start the business relationship as you mean to go on. Don't pile all the attention onto a prospective client before the sale and then abandon them as soon as they have signed on the dotted line. You will lose your customers as fast as your reputation. If you are employed don't cosy up to people when you need their help and ignore them when you don't, people will soon get wise and stop helping you.

2. Don't take on too much

The worst thing you can do is over promise and under deliver. If you do, these people will very quickly lose confidence in your abilities and will no longer trust your ability to come up with the goods.

3. Act with integrity

Be honest, fair and reliable. Don't take the easy way over the right direction. If you do a sloppy job, it will come back to haunt you.

4. Networking

i) Networking is a great way to build new business relationships that may prove invaluable in your current or future career, but networking needs to be done in the right direction. When you are networking, make sure that you listen to people and remember what they say.

You can refer to these things at a later date, and they will know you have paid attention to them and will feel you were genuinely interested in or valued what they had to say. People will remember you for this as all many people want to do talk about themselves.

ii) Notice how people communicate and try to mirror that so that they feel you are on a similar wavelength. Do it in a non-cynical and genuine way, and you will find that you'll have the ability to connect with people naturally? It's not about trying to CHANGE your personality to match theirs but instead finding and building on common ground.

Where are your personalities similar? Do you share any interests or points of view? We all behave differently with different people anyway; this is just about putting more thought into how you do it in a work environment. If you can make people feel comfortable with you, the easier and more productive that relationship will be.

iii) It's important to say thank-you, whether it's to someone thanking them for their business, to someone who has put some business your way or if someone has helped you in any respect.

We all like to be acknowledged and want to know that people

appreciate what we do rather than just taking it for granted. If someone has given you a referral, send a thank-you note and if appropriate, a gift. They will remember you over the people that don't do this and who do you think they will refer to in the future? It creates a win-win situation.

5. Compromise

Every relationship and business relationship needs give and take; if not resentment will build up if one party believes that the other always gets their way. Compromising is not a sign of weakness; it's quite the opposite if you're strong enough to publicly accept that you don't have the solutions to everything and that you realise the value and necessity of other peoples' contributions.

6. If things go wrong

Don't ever give anyone any ammunition to say that you have been unprofessional. Don't burn any bridges; you never know when previous contacts may come in useful. Always leave a business relationship on the best terms possible

7. Respect

Respect and acknowledge others rights to their opinions - even if they're not the same as your own

8. Help others to be successful, and they will help you

No man (or woman) is an island. We all need to build, develop and share our knowledge and skills within our networks. Partner with people who have the skills that you don't have. So much more can be achieved with others than could ever possibly be performed on our own.

9. Don't overestimate

A common mistake, (hey it is fun) is to beef up those revenue numbers on paper and post the low end for expenses. Try it the opposite, and you might be surprised.

If you still make money by dropping your revenue projection by 25% and increasing your expenses by 10%, then go for it, you have a winner.

10. Be protective of your time

Working for yourself, and worse, working alone, can become a mental challenge. There often seems to be some personal or social activity going on that can sway your concentration.

If you work from home, set some hours and keep them. Encourage others to wait for your attention. The more you do this, the less you have to do it!

11. Business boils down to relationships

Being genuine and honest in your approach will become what you are known for in business. Cheat or treat one customer unfair and believe me, the world will know about it. Whether you get rich or poor or something in the middle, if you have enjoyed your work, and worked with integrity, then you will always like yourself.

If you are ever in doubt as to how you should behave in your business relationships, then treat others the way you would like to be treated, and you'll usually find that's a great place to start!

Every action will cause a reaction. Make sure you know what you plan to accomplish with each phone call, sales letter or new purchase. Take a couple of minutes to understand your desired outcome, and you will be more inclined to reach your goal.

MONOGRAMMED NOTES AND PERSONALIZED STATIONERY

Whether you're a small or large business that is looking for a unique way to stand out among your competitors, turn to personalised stationery, with so many different options, such as monogrammed notes, personalized notepads, and individual business cards, there's bound to be something that fits your company's brand and personal style.

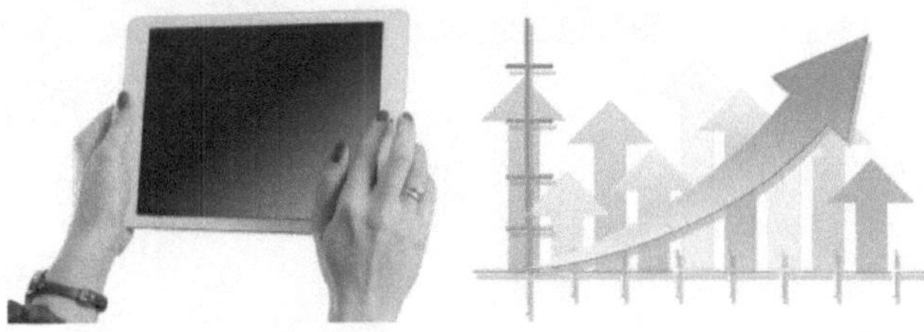

➢ **Send Business Correspondence Using Monogrammed Notes**

In this increasingly digital age, the art of the real note that arrives in the mail is a rarity. If you have a client that you want to thank personally, don't resort to an email message. Instead, use monogrammed notes and hand write your appreciation. The next time this client needs a product or service provider, this can help ensure that your company is at the top of the list.

Additionally, if you're sending holiday gifts or a present to celebrate the end of a challenging project, don't have them shipped directly from the company. Whether you're sending a gift basket full of treats or something to decorate the office, include handwritten monogrammed notes. This personal touch will help your gift stand out from any others, only because you took the time to write a quick note.

ADVERTISE WITH PRSNLIZD NOTEPADS

Nearly every business hands out personalised pens when they're trying to make an impression with their competitors. While these pens can be quite useful, they're everywhere, which means they can tend to blend into the background.

Instead of handing out pens, have some small, personalised notepads printed and give them out at your next trade show or send them to clients for a holiday or thank you gift. Because a notebook is in use in almost every office, you can help ensure that your company's name remains at the top of your clients' minds.

CRT ONE OF A KIND BUSINSS CRDS

Business cards are everywhere -- you probably have a stack of them sitting in a desk drawer yourself. However, if you're looking for a specific one, can you quickly pick it out of the heap? The chances are good that they blend, especially if they're boring white with a company's logo on the front. To help your card get noticed, use unique printing techniques, such as full-colour printing and die cuts.

These printing techniques can be more expensive than regular printing, though, which means many companies on a budget are hesitant to spend the money. If full-colour printing is too expensive, consider using a one colour printing process or a coloured cardstock to help your card stand out while sticking to your budget.

Whether you're looking for monogrammed notes, personalised notepads or one of a kind business cards, make sure that you're working with a printing company that's well-established, will send a proof of your product before it ships, and can provide you with a quick printing turn around. It will make sure that your finished product is one that you're proud to show off.

SIL MEDIA

If you started your business reasonably recently and you need to promote it using social media channels but are not sure exactly how to get started, there are several things that you can try, which may pay off. It will offer you tips to improve your social media interactions for great results.

Don't be intimidated by what you don't understand about social media

When you first start using social media channels to connect with people for your business, it may seem daunting and intimidating. You may feel even more that way if you have a small, intimate business. However, it is not nearly as frightening as you may think and you will begin to believe it once you start to use it.

From a financial perspective, it probably makes the most sense to learn how to use it yourself as opposed to hiring someone to do it for you because there is a high likelihood that you will have a limited budget when you first launch your business. You shouldn't worry because it is something that you can learn to do on your own. You will need to put in some time and effort (not to mention, a commitment to consistently devoting time each week to your social media interactions) but the cost will be a lot less than if you had to hire someone to do it for you.

When it comes to your social media interactions, with your goal of improving your business through those interactions, it is essential for you to understand how important it is for you to pay close attention to what you have online and to ensure that your content is always fresh and current. Here are some tips that you may find useful for your particular business:

➤ Pay close attention to metrics

Metrics (or analytics, as many people call them) are essential to your continued professional success. If you gather the parameters from your social media interactions and results of those interactions, you will have control (to a great extent) over how to drive your business.

The reason why that is true is that you will be able to identify trends and you will be able to determine where your social media interactions are paying off and where they are falling short. If you understand and can identify those concepts, you will have the power to change whatever isn't working, and you can fortify whatever is working well. Knowledge is power.

➤ Build a strong following

It is essential to have loyal followers who will sing your business's praises to other people whom they know and trust. However, as much as the loyalty factor is crucial, reaching out to a considerable quantity of people as a trade-off for acquiring top-quality loyal followers is not a worthwhile trade.

As is always the case, you need to start from the ground up with people with whom you are connecting online. You will not be able to do anything at all without establishing relationships. That has always been the case, and that will still be the case because that is how human beings operate.

➤ Manage your location

In many cases, it makes a lot of sense to interact online with other people who are in your general geographic area. One of the reasons why that make such good feeling is that you also have the opportunity to interact with those people in person. That may or may not happen, but it is good to know that it can happen quickly if you both want to build your relationship in that way. Of course, if some of your online connections are too far away to do that, you may wish to consider Skype, which almost feels like you are both in the same room.

➢ **Stick to a schedule**

It is imperative for you to write and post on a consistent basis. If you have a plan and you stick to that plan, you will probably find that you are accomplishing a lot more than if you write and post on the fly. Also, there may be some opportunities to automate the posting part, which will most likely make your life a whole lot easier.

Take advantage of the content that you have at your disposal: In many cases, it is vital to present fresh content. However, that doesn't mean that you can't also recycle content and curate content, if and when the situation is appropriate. There are several advantages to that, including providing content that is innovative and exciting for your readers and drawing from a bottomless pool of material. If you use that approach, it will take you a lot longer to run out of topics, ideas, etc.

Using social media for your business is necessary and very smart. Social media gives you so many advantages, and it will not take a lot of work for you to learn how to use and manage it effectively. Once you have gotten comfortable with interacting through your chosen social media channels, you will see the positive results to start happening.

One general piece of advice is that you should keep a careful watch on your social media channels and regularly determine if they still work for your business. It is essential to stay connected on a regular basis. After all, you are building relationships. Relationships needed to be nurtured and loved so that they flourish in the best way possible.

FINAL REMARKS

If you are running a business, buying a business, or growing business these low and no cost business practices will result in an excellent return on investment and usually all it takes to get these returns is to consider them and do them.

www.ingramcontent.com/pod-product-compliance
Lightning Source LLC
LaVergne TN
LVHW041811190726
843493LV00009B/2881